Grandpa Saturday: Kite Day

Charlie Schmerbauch

Drawings by: Theresa Bernhardt

JenAlice Publications
Grandpa Saturday: Kite Day

Published in the United States by JenAlice Publications
PO Box 576
Campo. California 91906

ISBN 978-0-9863891-0-8

This book is dedicated to our mothers:

Jennie J. Schmerbauch
July 15, 1923 – August 16, 2012

Alice E. Barna
December 4, 1925 – December 5, 2011

They worked so hard to make our lives better and in doing so made their lives great!

The 2nd Saturday of each month was Grandpa Saturday. Matt and his sister Jenna always spent that day with their Grandpa, their mother's father. It was almost always the best day of the month for them, because they did very different things with Grandpa than they did with their friends or mom and dad. He was very old, at least 60, and sometimes he made squeaky and grunty noises when he stood up, sat down, or bent over. But, he knew a lot of stuff and how to do and make things. He seemed happy to teach these things to his two grandchildren. They either made or learned something very interesting every time they came to visit.

They always had fun on Grandpa Saturday.

Mom pulled the van up in front of Grandpa's house, Matt and Jenna jumped out, then they turned to give mom a kiss and a hug. Eight-year-old Matt thought that this kissing and hugging was OK for a girl like Jenna who was only six, but he thought that it was very weak behavior for an older, almost grownup boy, like him. But, it made his mom happy, and as long as his friends didn't see him, he would do it.

"Have fun and I will be back at 5:00 to pick you up" said Mom as she drove away.

The big door of the garage was open at the end of the long driveway that went up beside the house. The gate that leads to the backyard where Grandpa has his big workshop was open too. It was a lot bigger garage than they had at home. It seemed like he had every tool there was, and it seemed that he could make almost anything. In the two garages there were all kinds of things stored on shelves, hanging from the ceiling, and sorted into little drawers and bins everywhere. There were tons of screws and little squiggly metal things that in Grandpa's words "might come in handy some day". He seemed to know where they all were, and when and where he had gotten them. He often bent them and cut them and drilled holes in them to make them do things that were different than they were designed to do when they were made.

Grandpa was standing at his table saw. Matt knew it was called a table saw, because he learned it last month, when they'd made birdhouses for the backyard birds at his and Grandpa's houses. They'd used it to saw the wood to the right sizes for the sides and bottom and top. There was a lot of noise and the sawdust was flying around, as Grandpa carefully pushed wood through the sharp spinning blade, using a push stick so his fingers would not get close to the blade. When Grandpa saw the kids coming up the driveway he turned off the saw and greeted them with his usual joking "Not you guys again!!" Jenna always frowned, but Matt knew it was just his way of kidding around with them.

Jenna asked, "What are you making?"

He said, "You mean, what are WE making. I think today is going to be Kite Day. I am sawing wood to use for the kite sticks".

Matt said, "My friend Jimmy has a kite that he bought at the store."

"Anyone can get a kite at the store", said Grandpa, "But I've always liked to make my own and I'm going to teach you two how to do it too if you want to learn? They both nodded yes.

"I was just a little older than you when I made my first kite, but I didn't have anyone to teach me"

"Then, how did you do it?"

"Well, I found a broken one. I measured it, and studied it and made one just like it. It wasn't too hard"

"My dad didn't have a table saw, but he went over to the high school and used the one in the woodshop classroom to make the sticks for me."

"Ok, where do we start" chimed the children in one voice. Matt was a little skeptical, but Grandpa always seemed to know how to do a lot of stuff, and kite making was probably one of those things.

"Well, I just finished sawing the sticks. It wasn't very hard, but the table saw is still a little too dangerous for you kids to use. The most important thing about kite sticks is that they be very strong and very lightweight. That means you first have to pick a piece of wood without any knots in it and very straight grain."

"What are knots and grain?" asked Jenna.

"Knots are where the little branches grow out of the big ones, usually the trunk, the big part of the tree that comes out of the ground."

"We know what the trunk is!"

"Well, you didn't know what knots and grain were. Anyway, knots are those round marks like this in the wood." Grandpa picked up a thin piece with a dark brown circle in it. "Grain is these lines in the wood that go from one end to the other"

"Here Jenna try to break it." Jenna took the wood with the dark circle from Grandpa and it broke almost before she tried.

"Now try to break it where there isn't a knot, where the grain lines go along the whole length of the stick."

She bent the wood and it just flexed. "Oh, I see it's very strong and light."

"Yep"

"For this kind of kite we cut one stick 36" long and the other 24" long." said Grandpa, as he handed the tape measure and pencil to Matt.

"This kind of kite?" asked Jenna.

"Oh yeah, there are lots of kinds of kites. People have been making kites for thousands of years. We're going to make the simplest and most common one, "the diamond" said Grandpa.

He had shown them how to use the measuring tape before. Matt hooked the end of the tape measure on one end of the stick; he made a little mark with a pencil at 36" and then used a little saw to cut the stick to the right length. He then handed the tape and pencil to Jenna and she marked another stick at 24" and handed it to Matt to cut off.

"This is a coping saw. It is used to make very fine and small saw cuts". Grandpa showed them how to make the little saw cuts on the end of one of the sticks.

Matt sawed the cuts into two more ends and Jenna did the last one. Grandpa tied the two sticks together like a cross and then put a string all the way around the ends of the sticks using the little saw cuts to hold it. He asked Jenna to put her finger on the string while he tied the knot.

Grandpa reached under his worktable and brought out some newspaper. It was the comics section from the Sunday paper with all the bright colors. They spread it on the floor in a clean place. And then glued 3 pieces together. They laid the kite frame on the paper and with a pencil. Grandpa marked a line around the diamond shaped kite frame with about 1" of extra space all the way around the outside. Then Jenna cut the paper on the line while Grandpa and Matt made a second kite frame.

With a little paste and her 1st grade knowledge of how to use it, Jenna expertly glued the paper around the strings. Then, together, they all completed papering the second kite.

It was now 12:15 and time for lunch. While the kids swept up the sawdust and put away the tools. Out on the patio, Grandpa got some hotdogs cooking on the gas grill. Grilled hotdogs are so much better than boiled ones. Matt got cold sodas from the refrigerator and they sat down to eat. Sodas and hotdogs were something Mom didn't think was so great about Grandpa Saturday. But, they all three thought, they sure tasted good outside under the warm sun.

After lunch, they collected the kites and balls of string, and then walked the three blocks to the park, near Grandpa's house. Jenna wanted to ride in Grandpa's funny colored van, but Grandpa said that he needed the exercise walking would give and it would be good for them too. Grandpa talked a lot about how kids did not get enough exercise "these days".

They tied the balls of string to the kites very tightly and they were ready. The wind was very strong at the park and they didn't even have to run with the kite to make it go right up, but then it started spinning round and round crazily until it crashed. Three more times it happened in exactly the same way, then Grandpa said, "Well, the wind is so strong today, it looks like we are going to need a stabilizer on the kite."

"What's a stabilizer?" asked Jenna. Matt was glad that she had asked before he had to ask, an 8 year old boy should probably know what a "stabilizer" was, he thought to himself.

"It's a fancy name for a tail" said Grandpa. "It will make the bottom of the kite a little heavier and keep it pointed downward so the kite won't swirl, twirl, and spin like that, and crash. We will put a little one on it first and if we need to, we can add more to it until it holds steady. One time when I was a boy, about 11 or 12, the wind was so strong that we had to tie a rock at the end of the tail to make it work!"

"Once we made a really big kite, taller than I am now, and it caught so much wind and it was pulling so hard that we tied the string to the schoolyard drinking fountain to keep it from pulling me away across the playground. But, the string kept breaking. So we cut the slits into the paper for some of the wind to pass through, and then it worked just fine. You have to learn to adapt to the conditions of the day. Other guys said, 'Oh there's too much wind, let's go home.' And they went. I was the only one that had fun kite flying that day".

Grandpa took an old piece of bed sheet out of his pocket and tore it into long strips about 2 or 3 inches wide and 2 feet long. He tied three of them together with big bows. He tied that onto the bottom of the kite. "Now, that's a good looking tail." He then handed the kite to Matt.

"Matt took off running letting out string as he went. Up, up, up went the little kite. The quivering tail made it stay straight up and down. Matt thought that that was very fine. Jenna thought that the tail made it very pretty. It was very high in the sky and pulling very hard on the string, as it wiggled in the strong breeze. The colors of the comics looked great with the sun shining through the thin paper.

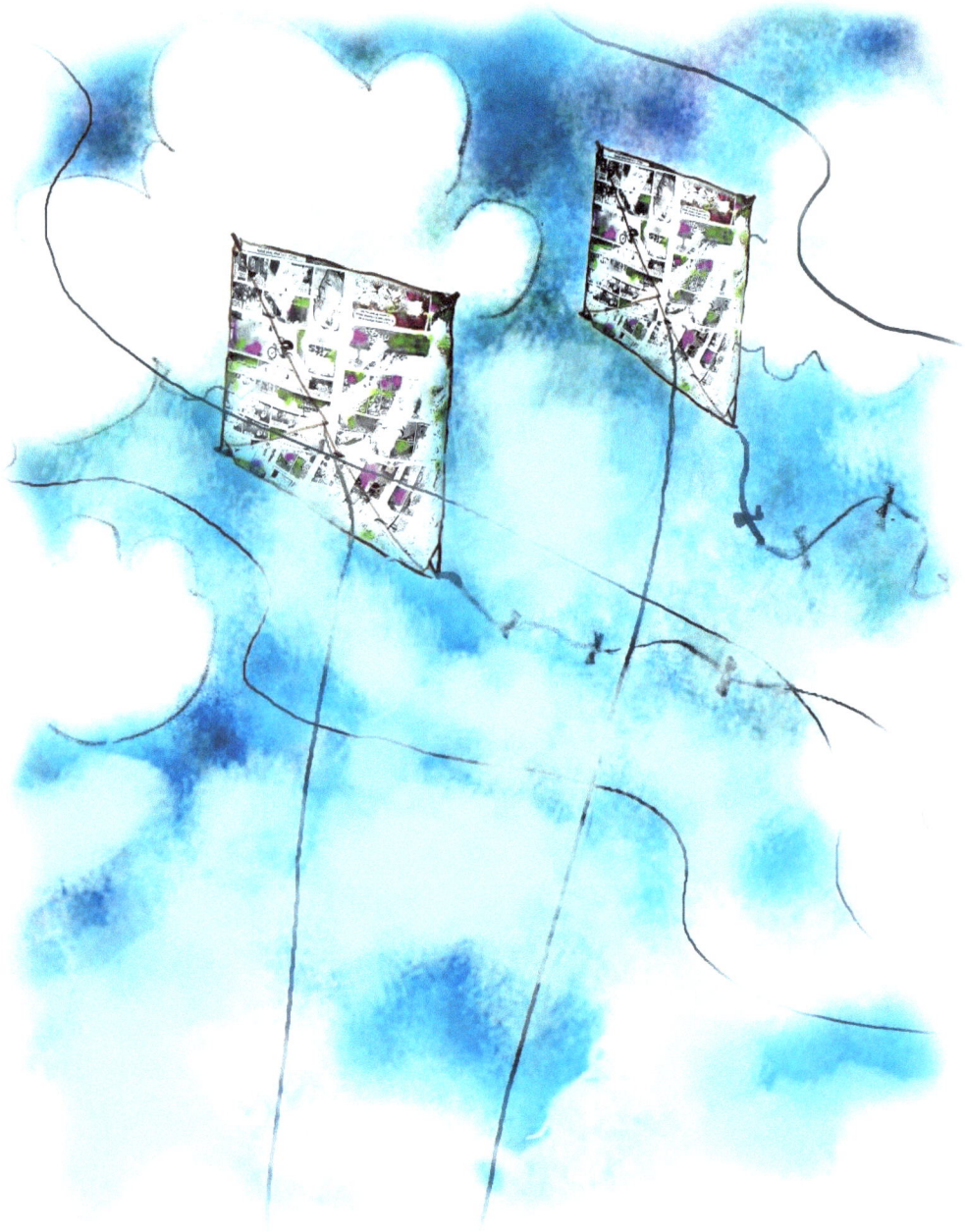

Matt handed the ball of string to Jenna and ran off to launch the other kite. Grandpa sat on the top of a picnic table with his feet on the seat with a very satisfied look on his face, while the kids laughed and giggled.

The kids did not want to leave when it was time, so Grandpa called Mom with his cell phone and arranged for her to pick them up at the park. That way they could stay a little longer flying the kites.

When Mom arrived she watched for a while, then the children put the kites into the back of her van. Jenna gave Grandpa a big kiss and hug, it was Matt's turn, but Grandpa reached out with his hand, and took Matt's hand and gave it a shake. Grandpa knew that boys did not go in for all that kissin' and huggin' stuff, but Matt sorta pulled a little on his arm and gave him a big hug. Matt knew that no matter how old he or Grandpa got, he would always have a hug for Grandpa.

"Now when you fly those kites at home don't do it in the street or where there are telephone wires or big trees. I don't want you calling me to climb up a tree to get your kite down, I'm kinda old and creaky to be climbin' a tree you know!!"

A lot of giggles were heard as the van drove away.

How to Make a Kite

Grandpas, or dads, or moms or big brothers or sisters this is a very easy project to do. The hard part is the thin sticks. If you do not have a table saw, try a neighbor. If that is not going to work, go down to the high school shop and have one of the students cut them for you. An alternate way to make sticks is to split a very dry bamboo into thin sticks.

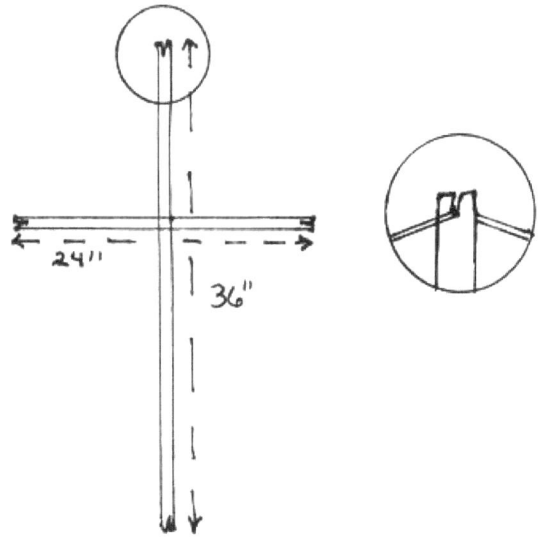

Illustration 1

You need them to be about $3/8^{th}$ of an inch wide and 5/32nd of an inch thick. Then cut one 36" long and one 24" long. The last work with a saw is a small cut on the end called a nock, kind of like the end of an arrow. This is just $1/8^{th}$ or $3/16^{th}$ deep where the string will go around the perimeter of the kite.

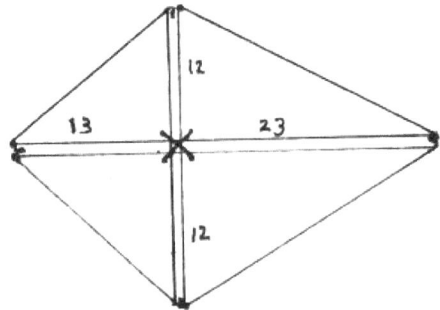

Illustration 2

Now for assembly: mark the 36" stick at 13", mark the 24" stick in the center at 12" this is where they will intersect. Tie the two sticks together into a cross where the marks meet. Go across the junction in both directions and tie a tight knot. Now put some string around the points of the sticks in the small cuts/nocks and tie the ends together in one of the long legs of the diamond shape that this makes.

Now for the paper: Since I was an eight year old, I always used the Sunday comics paper because it was colorful and free. But you can use Birthday or Christmas wrapping paper, or any light strong paper. Or you can glue together smaller pieces.

In any event, whatever you choose, lay it face down on the ground or table and put the kite frame on it. Draw a line around the whole thing allowing an extra 1 inch outside the string all the way around to fold over for gluing.

Cut on this line all the way around. Then cut a small scallop into the four corners of the paper for the stick ends.

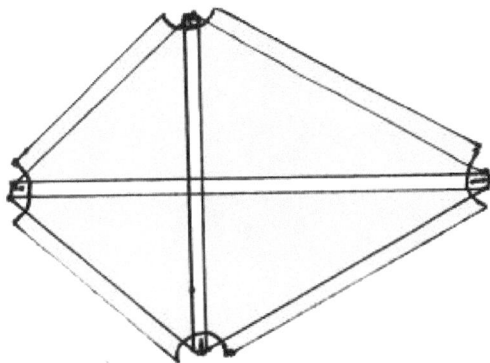

Illustration 3

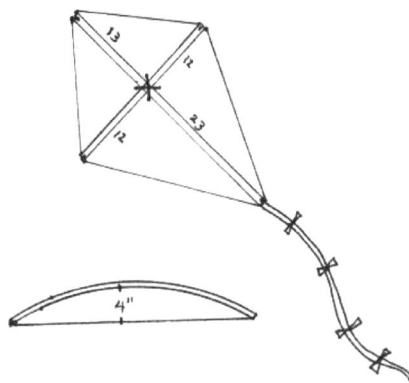

Illustration 4

Now glue the paper around the string using the 1" extra, to fold and wrap around the string and glue back on itself.

The next step is to bow the kite by tying a string to one end of the short stick and pulling it across the back of the kite to the other end of the short stick until the kite is bowed about 4 inches in the center. This will lend a little and necessary aerodynamics to the kite, allowing the wind slide around the kite

The bridle is next: poke a small hole in the paper 10" up and 15" down from the crossing point of the sticks, on the long stick. Poke a piece of string through the hole at the top and tie it to the vertical stick. Holding the center out from the kite about 10" tie the other end to the stick through the lower hole. The last step is to tie the end of the ball of string to the bridle and you are ready to fly. Hint: I like to put a piece of tape where the holes are in the paper and have the string go through a hole in the tape so it will be stronger and not rip the paper so easily.

Sometimes if the wind is too strong, as in the story, you need to put a tail on the bottom of the kite to keep it stable. 15 or 18-inch pieces of 2 or 3-inch wide cloth tied end to end with big bows (just for appearance sake) will usually do the job. Once I tied a big sock on. In a very strong wind, you may need to make it 6 or 8 feet long.

Good luck and have fun with the kids.

About the Author

Terri and I didn't meet until I was 62 years old and she 60, a big tragedy; we could have had 40 more years together. I have done a lot of different jobs, both white and blue collar. From age 6 to 18, I probably read 150 and sometimes 200 books a year. I got them from the school library, borrowed them from friends, and the library at the Boys Club. Now I'm older and have to work so that's down to about 50 or 60 a year. It was a way to travel the world, or go backward or forward in time right in your own room. It also was a great way to expand my vocabulary and gave me a wide knowledge of a lot of things and the ability to always know a little of what people were talking about. I always imagined that I could write books, now I'm 67 and this will be the first of many more, I hope.

I'm not sure I like coming after the chickens and goats in her bio!

About the Artist

   I've always loved to draw and paint. As a young artist fresh out of college I had the opportunity to work with author and educator Vick Knight Jr. on a children's book called "The Night the Crayons Talked". It was published in 1976. Since then, I have been creating art for my clients in mosaics, fabrics, paint and paper as well as designing landscapes throughout San Diego County. I now live and work in beautiful Campo, California enjoying chickens, goats, Charlie and the great outdoors.

   You can see more of my work at www.ArborStudios.com.

www.ingramcontent.com/pod-product-compliance
Lightning Source LLC
LaVergne TN
LVHW072109070426
835509LV00002B/92